Curses, Foiled Again!

A Play

Evelyn Hood

Samuel French – London
New York – Sydney – Toronto – Hollywood

FOR AMATEUR PRODUCTION ENQUIRIES

UNITED KINGDOM AND WORLD EXCLUDING NORTH AMERICA
plays@SamuelFrench-London.co.uk
020 7255 4302/01

Each title is subject to availability from Samuel French,

depending upon country of performance.

CHARACTERS

Kate (playing **Lucy**, the maidservant)
Henry (playing **Jasper Rotten**, the villain)
Sandra (playing **Nurse**, the old family retainer)
Peter (playing **Victor Pureheart**, the hero)
Anna (playing **Lady Flawless**, the elderly aunt)
Stephanie (playing **Nell**, the heroine)

Time—the present

CURSES, FOILED AGAIN!

The drawing-room of Lady Flawless' house. A rehearsal by an amateur dramatic group of a Victorian Melodrama is in progress

A door UR leads to the hall, and a door UL leads to the rest of the house. In the upstage wall there is a window R and a drinks table UC. A sofa is DRC and an armchair with a small table beside it DLC. A writing bureau and small chair stand DR. There is a shawl over the back of the chiar

As the CURTAIN rises Kate, dressed as Lucy the pretty maid, is putting paper cups on the small table

Henry, as Jasper Rotten, a handsome villain with a black moustache and wearing a cloak, enters R and tiptoes to Lucy who does not see him

Jasper Pssst!

Lucy (*jumping*) Oh, Mr Jasper, you did give me a fright!

Jasper Lucy, me lovely, I want you.

Lucy (*giggling*) Now, Mr Jasper, I've told you before—not when I'm working. You'll have to wait till my evening off.

Jasper Not that, you silly little—you dear little thing. I want your assistance. Lucy—how would you like to dress like a fine lady and have jewels to wear?

Lucy Oh—Mr Jasper! But that could never be!

Jasper Depend on me, Lucy. We're going to be rich!

Lucy But how, Mr Jasper?

Sandra, playing the old nurse, enters L without being noticed

Jasper leads Lucy to the front of the stage, Nurse lurks at the back of the stage, listening

Jasper My dear cousin Nell and my aunt, Lady Flawless, are on their way back from the solicitor's office at this ... (*He stops,* *looks over his shoulder. There is nobody there. He reverts to his normal voice)* Sandra!

Nurse (*in her normal voice*) Yes?

Jasper (*with heavy patience, not looking at her*) Where are you, Sandra?

Nurse I'm up here, eavesdropping.

Jasper I *told* you—you have to come right down here beside us.

Nurse But they'd see the nurse if she was right down beside them.

Jasper The Victorians didn't go in for reality, they went in for a sense of THEATRE! Right down here beside me.

Nurse comes down to him. He catches her wrist and pulls her to his side

You're supposed to stand so close that you could bite my ear.

Nurse Oh come on, darling, I think our ear-nibbling days are over, don't you?

Jasper Don't be coarse, Sandra. Now, where were we?

Lucy Er——

Nurse I was not-nibbling your ear.

Jasper (*glaring at her, he goes back to his Jasper voice*) My dear cousin Nell and my aunt, Lady Flawless, are on their way back from the solicitor's office at this very moment. I hurried on ahead of them to lay me plans. Nell has just been informed that she is sole heir to the fortune of our late uncle, Sir Silas Pureheart, and his vast wealth is to go to her alone.

Lucy Oh, what a shame, Mr Jasper. After you went to all that trouble to fix up the tripwire across the stairs for him, too!

Jasper But—I have a plan. If Nell should die I am to inherit her money. I could, of course, persuade her to sign this document ... (*he brings it from his pocket with a flourish then puts it back*) ... giving the money to me as a gift, but that would make her destitute, and I couldn't bear to see little Nell living in abject poverty.

Lucy You always did have a kind heart, Mr Jasper. (*She shakes a finger at him*) It'll be your undoing one day.

Jasper Better to kill her off and be done with it.

Nurse throws her hands up in horror

Lucy Another tripwire?

Jasper No, this time I intend to be a little more subtle.

Jasper, with a flourish, produces a large black bottle marked "Poison" from inside his cloak

Lucy Oh, Mr Jasper, wherever did you get that?
Jasper (*casually*) I always carry it with me in case of emergency.

Jasper crosses to the drinks table, bumping into Nurse

Nurse (*in her own voice*) Ow—my foot!

Nurse collapses on to the sofa

Jasper (*in his own voice*) For heaven's sake, Sandra!
Lucy (*in her own voice*) Are you all right?
Jasper You'll have to remember to step out of the way just before my move!

Nurse gets to her feet, and limps a few steps

Nurse (*sarcastically*) Sorry.
Jasper (*going to the drinks table; speaking in his stage voice*) I'm going to put this into the Madeira. I shall persuade dear Nell to drink some, and you, Lucy, will pour it for her. Then ... (*he pours the poison into the wine*) ... the deed will be done.
Lucy (*producing a letter from her pocket; in her stage voice*) What about this letter that has just arrived for Miss Nell? Should I give it to her before or after she dies?
Jasper Let me see that. (*He takes the letter from her*) Zounds! 'Tis from Victor Pureheart, the only child and true heir of Uncle Silas!
Lucy But surely your uncle's only child was kidnapped by the gypsies as an infant and left to die in the snow?
Jasper Apparently not. He says here that he is alive, and coming here this very day to claim his inheritance. Curses!
Lucy Shall I pour the poisoned Madeira away?
Jasper No, no, I'll get rid of him easily enough——

Peter, dressed as Victor Pureheart, puts his head round the door

Victor (*in his own voice*) Er, Henry—the caretaker says the let finishes at half-nine.

Jasper groans

Nurse Of course it doesn't finish at half-nine! I booked an extension for tonight.

Jasper (*in his own voice*) You'd better go and argue it out with him then, hadn't you?

Nurse exits offstage

And don't take all night!

Anna, who plays Lady Flawless, puts her head round the curtains

Lady Flawless (*in her own voice*) Can we have a cup of coffee while we're waiting?

Jasper (*savagely*) Why not? It's only a festival ... who cares about the cup ... or the salver ... or the original play award?

Lucy exits

Jasper sits on the sofa and sulks

Stephanie, dressed as Nell the pretty young Victorian heroine, enters. She is carrying two paper cups filled with coffee

Nell Here you are, Henry—this'll make you feel better.

Jasper (*taking a cup*) You think so?

Nell (*sitting beside him*) It's a super play. I think you're really clever to write it.

Jasper (*thawing*) Well—it just sort of comes naturally.

Nell I think Nell's a super part, really.

Jasper (*patting her hand*) Steph, you're what's known as a real little trouper.

Nell Am I?

Jasper (*lifting her hand and playing with her fingers*) Oh yes. Not much experience, but ... you don't have much experience, do you, Steph?

Nell No.

Jasper I could teach you such a lot.

Nell Could you, Henry?

Jasper Mmm. As a matter of fact, I've pretty well finished with this club. It's like an orange that's been sucked dry, you know? No challenge any more. I'm thinking of going to another group. Larger, not afraid to experiment. I could take you with me.

Nell Me?

Jasper Believe me, Steph, you and I could set the stage alight in the right sort of play. Like the play I'm writing at the moment.

This is just a little pot-boiler. I'd really like your opinion on my new script.

Nell Oh. Well . . .

Jasper Perhaps we could talk about it over a drink . . . say Friday?

Nell What would Sandra say?

Jasper Good lord, we're not married—we only live together. It's an open relationship. Besides, I'm just about ready to move on. I've out-grown Sandra.

Nell An orange that's been sucked dry?

Jasper More like a lemon. About Friday . . .

Nurse enters

Jasper lets go of Nell's hand quickly

Nurse (*eyeing them narrowly*) It's okay. He'd got his lets in a twist, that's all.

Jasper hands Nell the cup and rises, suddenly brisk

Jasper Right, everyone, panic over. Clear the stage, please!

Nell exits offstage

Lucy enters

Jasper, Lucy and Nurse take up their original positions

Lucy (*in her stage voice*) Shall I pour the poisoned Madeira away?

Jasper (*in his stage voice*) No, no—I'll get rid of Victor Pureheart in my own . . .

There is a pause

Ah! (*Aiming his words to the wings*) I *think* I heard a dog bark!

Victor barks off

(*Crossing to the window; in his own voice*) Try to bark on time tomorrow night, will you, Peter? (*Back to his stage voice*) They're back. Off to the kitchen, Lucy, while I open the door for them.

Jasper exits R

Lucy exits L

Nurse limps to the front of the stage to address the audience

Nurse (*in a strong cockney accent*) What a wicked plot! I always suspected that——

Jasper enters

Jasper (*in his own voice*) Sandra—what on earth are you doing?
Nurse (*as herself*) I'm being an old countrywoman.
Jasper Old countrywomen don't walk like Long John Silver and talk like a Pearly Queen.
Nurse I beg your pardon! My accent was complimented when I did *Pygmalion*!
Jasper *Pygmalion* was a long time ago.
Nurse It was also a very good play.
Jasper Look, if I was George Bernard Shaw I wouldn't be writing and directing for a third-rate amateur dramatic club, would I?
Victor (*off*) D'you think we could get on? The let finishes in thirty minutes.
Jasper Right! So do you think you could tone down the accent—darling?
Nurse (*sweetly sarcastic*) Of course—sweetheart.

Jasper exits

(*In a modified accent*) Mr Jasper was cruel, even in the nursery—but now I have proof. I will see to it that my dear Miss Nell is saved and that Mr Victor knows the truth about his cousin Jasper!

Nurse steps back as:

Lady Flawless enters, in jewels and silks. She is followed by Nell and Jasper

Lady Flawless Ring for the servant, Nell.

Victor barks off

Whatever is Frou-Frou doing out there?

Nell rings the hand-bell on the drinks table and goes to the window

Jasper (*fawningly*) My dear aunt—let me take your cloak—let me help you to your chair.

Jasper escorts Lady Flawless to the armchair. There is a pause

Nurse (*in her own voice*) It's you, Stephanie.
Nell (*in her own voice*) Is it? Oh, sorry. Er . . .
Nurse Frou-Frou . . .
Nell Frou-Frou . . . er . . .
Jasper . . . is savaging the coachman!
Nell Oh, yes. Sorry. (*Reverting back to her stage voice*) Frou-Frou is savaging the coachman, Aunt.
Lady Flawless But it is not his dinner-time! Nurse, go and take the silly man away from Frou-Frou at once.

Nell moves to the front of the stage and Nurse goes to the window

Nurse I fear it is too late, m'lady.
Lady Flawless How very tiresome. Jasper, hire another coachman tomorrow—a thin coachman. I will *not* have fat servants tempting dear Frou-Frou.

Lucy enters and takes the cloak from Jasper

Jasper Very well, Aunt.
Lady Flawless Tea, Lucy.
Lucy Yes, my lady.

Lucy exits; and returns at once with a cheap teapot, which she places on the table beside Lady Flawless

Lady Flawless (*in her own voice*) I hope we're going to get a proper teaset for tomorrow. Paper cups look silly in a Victorian drawing-room.
Lucy (*in her own voice*) Yes, of course. The thing is, Mummy just refuses to let me bring her good teaset to rehearsals.
Jasper (*curtly*) Can we get on, please? (*In his stage voice*) Cousin, your face is pale with sorrow. Pray be seated and the maid-servant will pour you a glass of Madeira.

Jasper leads Nell to the sofa then goes to the drinks table. Lucy goes to the table and Jasper watches closely as she pours a glass of wine. Nurse tries to take the decanter from Lucy and they tussle for it, then Jasper manages to catch Nurse in an armlock and tosses her aside. Nell and Lady Flawless are quite unaware of what is going on behind them

Nell (*during the fight; talking out front*) You are so kind to me, cousin Jasper. Er——

Jasper stops wrestling with Nurse

Jasper (*in his own voice*) If only Uncle Silas had shared his fortune ...

He goes back to the struggle

Nell (*in her own voice*) Oh yes. Sorry. (*As Nell*) If only Uncle Silas had shared his fortune between us. It seems so unfair that I should be wealthy and you should be a pauper.

Jasper (*through clenched teeth; breathless from his struggles*) My dearest Nell, your comfort is my only concern. (*In his own voice*) You don't need to struggle so hard, Sandra.

Nurse (*in her own voice*) I'm quite sure the Victorians would.

On the last word Nurse gets in a blow to the stomach and Jasper doubles up

Nell But of course you must continue to live here with us, instead of having to beg your bread in the gu ... gutter.

She breaks down and giggles

Jasper (*in his own voice*) Stephanie ...!

Nell (*in her own voice*) Sorry. It's just—bread in the gutter. It makes me feel like a ventriloquist.

They all look at her

Gread and gutter. Like a gottle of geer. Sorry.

Jasper I hate to be a killjoy, but we're appearing in front of an audience tomorrow night. If we don't want to make complete fools of ourselves we'll have to concentrate on what we're supposed to be doing!

Nell Sorry.

Lucy hands the wine to Jasper and exits L

Nurse tries again to get at the glass. Jasper kicks Nurse in the shin. She hops about in agony

Nurse Ow!

Jasper Did I kick you too hard? Sorry.

Jasper isn't and Nurse knows it

(*Reverting back to his stage voice*) You're too kind, cousin.

Nell (*in her own voice*) It's me, isn't it? Er ... oh, help ... (*She takes the script from her bodice*) If I could just use my script just now I promise I'll know it by tomorrow night.

Lady Flawless (*in her own voice*) That's what you've been saying for the past three months, Stephanie.

Nell (*tears in her voice*) I have tried!

Jasper (*in his own voice*) Yes, she has. And as this is her first major part——

Nurse *That's* a major part?

Jasper Not as big as Eliza Dolittle, of course—but this play has just as much meaning as *Pygmalion*, in its own little way.

Jasper takes the script from Nell and is about to put it back into her bosom, then realizes what he's doing and gives it to her

Put the script away, Steph.

Nell But——

Jasper You'll learn better without it. Put it away, there's a good girl, and let's get on with the bloody rehearsal!

Nell does as she is told

Jasper Now—to think that if the real son and heir—

Nell Oh, yes. Isn't it funny how you know it at home, but when you get on to the stage it all sort of fizzles away?

Nurse Oh, terribly funny. Isn't it, Henry?

Jasper glares at Nurse

Nell (*in her stage voice*) Er—to think that if the real son and heir, Victor, hadn't been taken away by gypsies as an infant he would have inherited everything instead of me! (*An unpleasant thought strikes her*) You don't think he could still be alive, do you, Aunt?

Lady Flawless Not at all, child, everyone knows that he was left in the cold snow to die. That's what gypsies always do with kidnapped infants.

Jasper Here is your wine, cousin.

Nell (*taking the glass*) Thank you, Jasper.

Nurse limps hurriedly forward

Nurse Miss Nell ...

Nell What a pretty colour this wine is, Jasper.

Jasper Indeed it is. Drink it up before it gets cold.

Nurse (*agitated*) Miss Nell, there's something I must tell you before you——

Jasper (*loudly*) I mean, drink it up before it goes flat. Wine should always be drunk quickly.

Nell Really? In my book on etiquette for young ladies it recommends that wines should be sipped delicately and savoured on the tongue.

Nurse Miss Nell——!

Jasper Not Madeira. It must be swallowed in one draught.

Lady Flawless Talking of draughts, would someone get my shawl? (*She indicates the shawl, over the back of the small chair*)

Nurse Miss Nell——!

Nell Really, Nurse, I do declare you've become the most tiresome old chatterbox today. What is it?

Jasper Drink your Madeira, cousin.

Nell obediently raises the glass to her lips

Nurse Oh ... Miss Nell, I implore you ... don't ... you mustn't ...

Nell Oh dear, she's too overcome to make any sense. Here, Nurse, have a sip of my wine to clear your head.

Nurse ⎱ (*together*) No!
Jasper ⎰

Nell Oh—you're right—Madeira must be drunk in one draught. Drink it all down, Nurse.

Before Jasper can stop her Nell has poured her wine down Nurse's throat

Jasper (*in an aside*) Oh—curses!

Nurse goes into a dying scene, watched with fury by Jasper and with surprise by Nell. Lady Flawless looks on impassively, until Nurse reels towards the chair that holds the shawl

Lady Flawless That's right—over there.

Nurse reaches out, almost grasps the chair-back where the shawl lies, then reels the other way

Lady Flawless No, no—over *there*!

Finally Nurse collapses on the floor behind the sofa

Nurse (*in her own voice*) Oh God, I think I've fractured my coccyx!

Jasper (*in his own voice; martyred*) Sandra, there's a time limit in this festival, so don't take too long to die. (*He suddenly notices where she is*) What do you think you're doing?

Nurse (*in her own voice; from behind the sofa*) I'm dead.

Jasper You're really determined to undermine this play, aren't you?

Nurse No, I'm *trying* to make it look good in front of an audience.

Jasper I told you to die down stage front.

Nurse (*sitting up*) If I do, they'll be so busy watching to see if I breathe that they'll miss your wonderful meaningful dialogue. Besides, I can prompt Stephanie from here.

Lucy (*in her own voice*) If you're going to turn this into a domestic squabble I might as well go home.

Lady Flawless Me too.

Victor (*off; in his own voice*) Wait a minute—I haven't even been on yet!

Jasper (*stiffly*) Right, Sandra, have it your own way. Just have the courage to own up when the adjudicator blames me for bad positioning.

Lady Flawless Thank you. (*In her stage voice*) Nell, whatever is Nurse doing?

Nell trips lightly over to investigate

Nell She's lying down, Aunt.

Lady Flawless And why, pray, is she lying down on my drawing-room carpet?

There is a pause. Everyone looks at Nell

Nell (*in her own voice*) Oh, help . . .

Nurse (*from behind the sofa*) What . . .

Nell What?

Nurse . . . does . . .

Jasper Stop messing about, Sandra!

Nurse (*sweetly*) Sorry. "What does it mean . . ."

Nell I can't hear you.

Jasper She can't *hear* you, Sandra!

Nurse Oh, dear. Well, perhaps I can semaphore, like this—

Her feet appear over the back of the sofa, waving about

Jasper Now look here, Sandra ...

Lady Flawless (*in her own voice*) Can we get on? I'm picking Bill up at eleven, and he hates to be kept waiting. He's being difficult enough about all these extra rehearsals——

Jasper (*through his teeth*) "What does it mean when people ..."

Nell (*in her own voice*) Oh, yes. Sorry. (*She goes to look at Nurse; reverting to her stage voice*) Jasper, what does it mean when people stop breathing?

Jasper According to the latest medical findings, cousin, it usually means that they are dead.

Nell Oh. Nurse is dead, Aunt.

Lady Flawless Very thoughtless of her. Servants should die in the attic or the kitchens; not in the drawing-room when afternoon tea has just been served. Come, Nell, you shall assist me to change into some of my less formal jewellery before we take tea.

Nell Yes, Aunt.

Lady Flawless and Nell exit, stepping over Nurse's legs

Jasper paces

Jasper Confound the woman, she's ruined me plan. But I shall still succeed.

He reaches the window, and looks out

Curses! This handsome young man approaching the door must be Victor Pureheart!

The doorbell rings

Lucy passes through on her way to the front door

Jasper Delay him for a moment, Lucy, while I don my disguise.

Lucy Yes, Mr Jasper.

Lucy exits R to the front door

Jasper fumbles in his inside pocket

Jasper Luckily I always carry a disguise with me for such ... (*He reverts to his own voice*) Oh, God, where's the wig? Sandra, what did you do with the wig?

Nurse (*sitting up*) What do you mean, what did I do with it? It's your prop.

Jasper (*going through his pockets*) It was in the box in the kitchen. You said you'd see to the box.

Nurse (*getting to her feet*) Then presumably it's still in the box. Or the car.

Jasper Go and look in the car, then. Anna, have a look in the prop box. Kate, try the make-up box. Steph, help me look in the dressing-room ...

Jasper, Nell, Lucy and Lady Flawless exit in different directions

Left alone, Nurse shrugs, sighs and starts to go offstage

Victor, dressed as a handsome young Victorian hero, comes hurrying on behind her, grabs her, swings her round and kisses her

Nurse (*struggling free*) Get off, Peter! Somebody'll see us!

Victor Let them. A good-going scandal would be a sight more dramatic than this.

Nurse You're insulting the play Henry loves.

Victor I've had to stand back there listening to him insult the woman I love!

Nurse Don't be silly. And don't let Henry bother you, he's only doing his "harassed director" bit.

He advances, she backs away

Now, Peter ...

Victor I've been stuck in the wings, longing to kiss you—this has been the most frustrating evening of my life!

Nurse Won't be long now.

Victor You mean—you've decided to leave him?

Nurse No, I mean we've almost reached your entrance.

Victor Sandra, I can't stand by and let you be bullied any longer.

Nurse He's just uptight. This is the first play he's ever written.

Victor And Shakespeare it ain't. To hear him you'd think every word was a precious stone instead of a hulking great boulder.

Nurse I know. Poor Henry.

Victor Poor! I suppose you know that he's about to be unfaithful to you?

Nurse Stephanie? I know she's getting Henry's version of the casting couch technique, but he doesn't mean it. He's feeding his vanity, that's all. He'd run a mile if she took him seriously.

Victor (*taking a step towards her*) I need you, Sandra ...

Nurse No—he needs me. You just want me. I'd better find his wig and let you get some rehearsal.

She moves to the side of the stage, he blocks her way

Jasper (*off*) Sandra?

Victor turns aside as:

> *Jasper enters*

Nurse Good—you found it. In the prop box, was it?

Jasper Sometimes, Sandra, your voice gets right up my nose.

Nurse What a horrible thought.

She lies down behind the sofa

Jasper Clear the stage.

> *Victor glares at Jasper and exits*

> Right, everyone . . . (*He switches back to his stage voice*) Luckily I always carry a disguise about with me . . .

He whips a grey beard and wig from his inside pocket and dons them. He becomes elderly and doddery

> *Lucy ushers Victor in*

Lucy Mr Victor Pureheart.

Jasper Good-evening, young sir. I am Ambrose Linkpen, solicitor's clerk. Can I be of service to you?

Victor I am Victor Pureheart, long-lost heir of the late Sir Silas Pureheart, and I have come to claim my inheritance.

Lucy gasps and puts a hand to her mouth

Jasper You may go, Lucy.

Lucy Yes Mr Ja . . . sir.

> *Lucy exits*

Jasper Your inheritance? Alas, young sir, I regret that there is no inheritance. I am here to inform Miss Nell that Sir Silas Pureheart gambled the entire fortune away and died a poor, ruined man. So you might as well leave this unhappy house now.

Jasper opens the door

Victor But now that I am here, I must meet my relations again.

Jasper Your dear defunct departed pa not only died, sir, he died in dire debt which must be paid off. If you——

Nurse (*from behind the sofa*) Henry, I still think that speech makes you sound like the master of ceremonies at an Old Tyme Music Hall.

Jasper (*ignoring her*) If you take my advice, I say, you will leave at once, and rid yourself of such an unpleasant inheritance.

Victor Leave, at such a time? Never! I will toil until the end of my days, if need be, to pay off my father's debts. Kindly inform my aunt, Lady Flawless, that I am returned home at last.

Jasper (*to the audience*) Curse this man's upright honesty! (*To Victor*) Her ladyship is not at home, sir. Everyone is out but your cousin, Jasper Rotten.

Victor Then kindly fetch my cousin.

Jasper If you insist.

Jasper exits L

Victor follows him to the door, then turns and begins to walk to the centre of the stage. Before he has taken two steps:

Jasper enters behind him without his disguise

Jasper Forgive the delay, but Mr Linkpen had to tell me the full story of your sudden appearance. He has his doubts as to your claims, sir.

Victor Jasper, don't you remember me? Don't you recall the days when we shared the same baby carriage? The afternoon you threw me from it and hit my chubby little fingers with your rattle as I clung to the hood for my very life?

Jasper Sentimental stories do not prove that you are Victor Pureheart. Without proper proof I must ask you to leave this house of mourning immediately.

Jasper goes to the door and opens it with a flourish

Victor I have that proof—and I shall reveal it to the solicitor, Mr Ambrose Linkpen.

Jasper Oh—very well!

Jasper exits L

Victor follows him to the door, turns, and is startled when:

Jasper enters immediately behind him disguised as Ambrose Linkpen, his wig on the wrong way round

After lengthy discussion, your cousin and I have agreed that you are an imposter, sir. (*He points to the door with a flourish of the arm*) Kindly leave!

Victor Why is your hair back to front?

Jasper (*clapping his hand to his head; recovering his dignity*) Old houses can be very draughty. Now—show me your proof or leave forever, sir!

Victor I will gladly give you proof—but first, I must see my cousin Jasper again.

Jasper (*to the audience*) Is this man trying to drive me mad? (*To Victor*) One moment.

Jasper makes another quick exit and entrance; he is noticeably tiring

You wish ... (*He realizes he is using Mr Linkpen's voice and corrects it*) ... you wish to see me?

Victor You and Mr Linkpen both.

Jasper Together?

Victor Together.

Jasper (*to the audience*) The cunning fiend! Now what am I to do?

Lady Flawless enters, followed by Nell

Lady Flawless Jasper, who is this gentleman, pray?

Victor I am Victor Pureheart, only child and long-lost heir of Sir Silas Pureheart ...

Nell gasps

... and I have returned to the bosom of my family.

He kisses Lady Flawless's hand

Nell (*melting*) Oh—how exciting!

Victor And you must be little Nell.

He kisses Nell's hand. There is a pause

And you must be little Nell.

He kisses Nell's hand again

Nurse (*from behind the sofa*) "But Victor ..."

Nell Oh ... sorry ... (*Back to her stage voice*) But, Victor, you were stolen by the gypsies when only an infant, and left in the cold snow to perish.

Victor leads Nell to the sofa and sits beside her

Victor Fortunately I was kidnapped in July, so I escaped with a mild case of sunburn. A poor woodcutter found me and raised me as one of his own family. I only recently discovered my true name.

Lady Flawless Young man, the real son and heir had a birthmark.

Victor I still have it, Aunt.

Nell Where, where? Show it to us at once, Victor.

Lady Flawless He is sitting on it.

Nell (*overcome with maidenly embarrassment*) Oh!

Lady Flawless Come with me, young man. I am an old woman and I have travelled far and seen the seven wonders of the world, so I am quite unshockable. You shall prove to me that you are indeed the long-lost heir.

Victor Gladly, Aunt.

Victor rises to follow Lady Flawless out, then sees Nurse

Why, it is my dear old Nurse. What is amiss with her?

Jasper (*gloomily*) She drank too much.

Victor Alas. I have heard that it often happens with elderly retainers.

Victor and Lady Flawless exit

Jasper (*to the audience*) My plans are almost wrecked. But I can still triumph.

There is a pause

(*In his own voice; with restrained irritation*) It's you, Steph.

Nell ... er ...

Jasper (*loudly*) Oh, Jasper ...

Nell (*in her own voice*) Oh yes. Sorry——

Nurse (*standing up*) Look, Stephanie, don't keep saying you're sorry. Just learn the bloody lines! Or at least learn to take a prompt properly!

Nell gasps

Jasper Now calm down, Sandra——

Nurse All I'm asking is that Stephanie tries to behave like a member of the team, and not someone who just happened to be passing by at the time.

Nell Right—I've put up with your snide, jealous remarks for long enough!

Lucy, Lady Flawless and Victor appear from the wings

Nurse Jealous?

Nell Yes, jealous——

Jasper Steph——!

Lucy Come on—the let's nearly over!

Nell Jealous because I'm younger than you are, and jealous because you're a squeezed-out orange and you've lost Henry!

Victor That's enough, Stephanie!

Lady Flawless More than enough!

Nurse Hah! If losing him was *that* easy, I'd have managed it three or four girls ago.

Nell What do you mean?

Nurse (*clapping a hand to her head*) Stephanie, do you have to have everything pre-digested? You ... are ... not ... the ... first.

Nell But—Henry——?

Jasper (*hastily*) We're supposed to be rehearsing a play!

Lady Flawless Yes. Come on, Stephanie——

Nell No, I want to know what she meant.

Victor Why not? If you ask me, this is a sight more interesting than this ridiculous play.

Lucy Peter ...!

Jasper Listen mate, I've written a highly amusing send-up of Victorian melodrama, and if you didn't want us to stage it you should have said so at the first reading.

Victor With you sitting there waffling on about your brain-child and what it would mean to you to see it on-stage? You'd have burst into tears if we'd turned it down.

Jasper Since we're being honest, why don't you admit that you went along with it because you wanted to please Sandra? I've seen you whispering to her in corners! Well let me tell you something, sonny boy—Sandra and me don't split up that easily!

Victor Don't you talk about Sandra as if she was a sex object!

Nurse Oh, for heaven's sake let's all grow up!
Nell But Henry, you said we could set the stage on fire!
Jasper Shut up, Steph!

She gapes at him, then wails

Victor And don't talk to Stephanie as if she was an idiot!
Nell Oh—Peter!

She sobs on his shoulder

Lady Flawless ⎫   ⎧ If we're not going to rehearse I might
              ⎬ *(together)* ⎨ as well go and collect Bill——
Lucy ⎭   ⎩ Don't let's start arguing on the
                               night before the festival——

Jasper (*above them all*) All right—all right!

They all stop and look at him

Forget the festival!
Lucy But you can't forget a festival!
Jasper I can. I'll tell them we've all got the plague. I'm sorry I ever
forced you to do this lousy play.
Victor (*awkwardly*) I didn't say it was lousy——
Nurse (*coldly*) You as good as said it.

Jasper turns away and goes downstage

Jasper (*his voice beginning to shake*) We should have gone for the
Harold Pinter. I've ruined everything for the entire club. I've
been selfish and ... and ...

*He chokes to a standstill. Nurse watches him, but the others look at
each other, appalled. Nell goes to him*

Nell (*putting a hand on his shoulder*) Henry—come on, we like
your play.

*Jasper shakes his head, a broken man. They all, except Nurse,
clamour to do the play, surrounding him. Nurse stays where she is,
alone*

Jasper (*finally*) You mean it?

They reassure him

(*Turning to Nurse*) What do you think, Sandra?

Nurse goes to him, and takes his face between her hands

Nurse The usual thing, Henry. I think you're a piece of bread that always lands jammy side up. (*She kisses him briefly*) Let's get on with the play.

He looks at her for a moment, then snaps back into his old self

Jasper Right, everyone—where were we?

They hurry back to their respective places

And this time we keep going, right to the end. Let's get a sense of Theatre into this show!

Nell . . . er . . . ah! (*In her stage voice*) Oh, Jasper, what a handsome young man Victor is!

Jasper (*taking the large document from his pocket*) You think so? Cousin, I want you to write your pretty little name on this most unimportant scrap of paper.

Nell What is it?

Jasper A contract to have the house repainted.

Nell snatches the document from Jasper and moves down stage as she reads it

Nell What does relinquish and unreservedly mean?

Jasper (*airily*) They are but colours.

Nell If you chose them, Jasper, I'm sure they are very pretty.

Jasper (*leading her to the writing bureau*) Here is a quill, cousin. Sign the contract now, while we are alone.

Nell Very well.

Nell is about to sign when Victor bursts into the room, followed by Lady Flawless

Victor Stop!

Nell gives a faint scream and drops the paper and quill

Jasper (*to the audience*) A thousand curses!

Victor Sign nothing, Nell. Our wicked cousin is trying to trick you into handing over your fortune to him!

Jasper (*wildly*) A lie, a lie! How could you know that?

Victor (*coldly*) I have just looked at the script.

Nell Oh, Jasper—how could you?
Jasper You win, Pureheart—but I shall never be brought to justice—never! (*In his own voice*) I'll do the dog, right?

Jasper, laughing loudly, rushes from the room

Dog yapping interspersed with Jasper's cries are heard off

Nell rushes to the window, while Lady Flawless checks that all the tea things are on the table

Victor Shall I follow him?
Nell Too late—Frou-Frou has caught him.
Lady Flawless I always knew that Jasper would go to the dogs one day.
Victor (*leading Nell down front*) Pray avert your eyes, cousin—'tis not a pretty sight.
Nell Cousin? Then this is——
Lady Flawless This is indeed the long lost heir.
Victor (*to Lady Flawless*) And you are indeed my long lost Aunt.
Lady Flawless Aunt? No—for Sir Silas Pureheart and I were not, as everyone thought, brother and sister. We were husband and wife. He was a strangely eccentric man.
Victor Mother!
Lady Flawless My son!

They fall into each other's arms

Nell (*to the audience*) What a touching scene! It quite makes up for the sadness of Jasper's betrayal and dear old Nurse's death. And now I am no longer an heiress, but a poor girl who must earn her own living.
Victor (*going to her*) Never! Now that I have claimed my true inheritance I ask you, Nell, to share my wealth, my life and my name.

Victor kisses Nell's hand as Lady Flawless starts to pour tea

Nell (*rapturously happy*) Oh, Aunt—hasn't this been a most interesting day?

Jasper appears at the window

Jasper (*in his own voice*) Right—hold it just like that.

The three of them hold the pose, Lady Flawless with the teapot, Victor kissing Nell's hand

Fade lights . . .

The Lights begin to fade

And—curtain! Now—this is what I call a real sense of Theatre!

CURTAIN

FURNITURE AND PROPERTY LIST

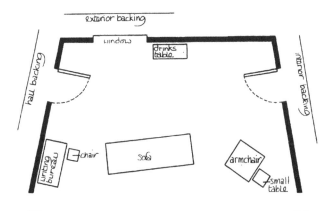

On stage: Drinks table. *On it:* decanter of Madeira, glasses and a small
   hand bell
   Sofa
   Armchair
   Small table
   Writing bureau. *On it:* quill
   Small chair. *On it:* shawl
   Paper cups

Off stage: 2 paper cups filled with coffee (**Nell**)
   Teapot (**Lucy**)
   Grey beard and wig (**Jasper**)

Personal: **Jasper:** document
   Jasper: large black bottle marked "Poison"
   Lucy: letter
   Nell: script

LIGHTING PLOT

To open: Full general lighting

Cue 1   **Jasper** "Fade lights ..."   (Page 22)
           The lights begin to fade

EFFECTS PLOT

Cue 1   **Jasper:** ". . . must be Victor Pureheart!"   (Page 12)
        The doorbell rings